MAGIC OF THE WILDERNESS

MAX ALBERT WYSS

MAGIC
OF
THE
WILDERNESS

A STUDIO BOOK · THE VIKING PRESS · NEW YORK

© Copyright 1969
by Verlag C. J. Bucher AG

English-language translation
Copyright © 1973
by Maureen Oberli-Turner

Layout and design: Edmund Amstad

Published in 1973
by The Viking Press, Inc.
625 Madison Avenue, New York,
N.Y. 10022

First published in Canada by
The Macmillan Company of Canada
Limited

SBN 670-44996-2

Library of Congress catalog card
number: 72-91831

Printed and bound in Switzerland

MAGIC OF THE WILDERNESS

Every journey which man makes to areas which neither natives nor foreigners have succeeded in conquering must of necessity lead not only beyond the borders of civilization but back into the past as well. Perhaps this is the real reason for such journeys—the urge to return to the elemental primitiveness of life in its natural state. Impenetrable jungles, barren steppes, and unexplored rivers are all symbols of a lost paradise, a paradise in which the lion is still king of the beasts and man still stalks his prey with bow and arrow. Our name for this paradise is the wilderness, and although I find myself unable to explain the concept to the reader, the pictures in this book may serve to conjure up its magic.

There is an almost uncanny power inherent in this magic, an allure that incites many a thoughtless traveler to set out on a hazardous adventure in ignorance of the limits of his mental and spiritual resistance, only to be laid low by the force of this primeval power. Thus the story is told of a young Swede in the 1930s who failed to return to the plantation from a Sunday hunting trip in Kenya and vanished into the bush with a rifle, a bearer, and a load of canned food; perhaps he had heard the legend of the elephants' burial ground.... Be this as it may, he reappeared three months later, exhausted, feverish, and confused, only to disappear again after no more than five paydays. A fool, said the Englishmen, though not without a certain admiration. A similar case was that of a doctor whose first acquaintance with the steppe and its wild life led him to give up his practice and his family, acquire a car and a tent, and find his happiness by adopting the life of a nomad. It was probably not so much the idea of being able to build a new existence in the wild west of Canada as the wanderlust of a frustrated pioneer that drove a friend of mine into the wilderness, from which he returned after long months of lonely journeying, physically exhausted, but freed from his inner burden of unrest. His

Entrance to the gorge of Akaui
on Nuku Hiva, Marquesas Islands

experience with wild forests and boundless prairies, confrontations with bears which surprised him in his sleeping bag at night, and his acquaintance with hunger and thirst had, to quote his own words, proved him to himself. Then there were the three irresponsible young men, the worry of their parents' lives, who returned from a foolhardy journey to Lapland, hitchhiking and on foot, to tell of living on raw fish and of being obliged to earn their return journey by working as woodcutters: in short, the wilderness had made men of them. But the wilderness does not lie before our doorstep, and it is not every young person who has the chance to work off his excess energy in the jungle. However, where there is a will there is usually a way.... From time immemorial their experience in the wilderness has compelled men to try to do it justice in writing, as if to overcome its enchantment by the magic of words, to break the spell by describing it. But the power of words is not given to everyone, and far more people are blessed with a fresh and unprejudiced way of seeing than with literary talent. Thus it is that the picture, complemented by the word, is capable of conjuring up the irretrievable moment in a visual form. But does this wilderness really still exist? For those who are capable of listening, seeing, and feeling, the answer is yes: it exists in a flight over the green hell of the Brazilian jungles, in the loneliness of the tundra, in the breath of tropical fragrance, and in the pulsing of jungle drums... barely an hour's march away from the camp to which winged giants can bear us, continents and centuries away!

THE GREAT SILENCE

On April 23, 1925, a man named A. F. Tschiffely, a Swiss by birth and a teacher by profession, started out on horseback on a journey that was to take him through the two Americas and last two and a half years: ten thousand miles in the saddle, in tropical heat and bitter cold, through jungles and prairies, past wild, rapid waters, insidious quagmires, and yawning abysses, over breathtaking mountains and across suffocating plains, with fever and thirst as his companions and the saddle for his pillow. His account of this journey is written in the somewhat cautious language of a man who sees things in a sober, realistic light, with the seemingly cold objectivity which is so well suited to genuine travel experiences; nevertheless, from time to time he has recourse to word pictures which reveal his high degree of sensitivity: "The first cry of a night bird pierced the silence, and now and then the ugly, cough-like bark of a roving fox could be heard...." Time and time again the "passionate traveler" has been moved and fascinated by the great silence of the primeval forest, a silence that can result in a peculiar keenness of hearing. Alexis de Tocqueville, for example, wrote as follows about his fellow traveler on a journey to the forsaken North American wilderness approximately one hundred years before Tschiffely's expedition: "He holds his breath and listens, in order to pick up the faintest sound of life."

The great silence of the wilderness which still exists in the dark depths of many a continent, in the unexplored interiors of tropical islands, in the icy tundra and on the flanks of unclimbed mountains, is the haunt of mystery and danger. The survival of the natives is dependent even today on their instinct and intuition, which, after all, are based on centuries of experience. Many an explorer owes the discovery of rare game to his ability to listen and to recognize the sounds and signs of nature which he learned from the natives. And the call of the wilderness, once experienced, is not easily forgotten.

THE PICTURES:

Page 9   Savanna in East Africa
Page 10   River landscape in India
          after the monsoon rains
Page 11   Brazilian jungle
Page 12   Tropical mountain forest
          at dusk

The great silence of the tropical night, which drives cattle into the kraal and men to the protection of the campfire, awakens the ancient fear of darkness and wild beasts. The cold stillness of dawn is dispelled by winds that spring up and surge like water over flanks of huge mountains, through the depths of inestimable forests, to the brink of the sea. The silver heron stands motionless in the blue dusk, and pink clouds of flamingos, unreal as illusions, keep watch over unseen waters. Blue-tinged clouds rise up to the sun over boundless, fiery red plains, the air is purged by the silent grayness of a storm, and leaping, flickering fires rage through the night....

And now, as the trees tremble in the wind and the stillness is shattered by the leap of a fish, the sudden movement of a fugitive animal, or the call of a solitary bird, life awakes in the depths of the forest. Or were our senses not sufficiently alert to recognize the strange, unknown sounds which were in fact there all the time, suppressed and distant? Is that the footfall of an antelope? Is that the gray shadow of an elephant in the darkness of the copse? Is that the acrid odor of a wildcat on the wind? Silence. And again: the crackle of dry twigs, the bark of a startled monkey, the strident call of a bird, a strangled cry.... Silence.

There was a time when the courage and hunting skill of a white planter in Africa were seriously in doubt if he failed to bring back at least the antlers of a kudu, the skin of a giant snake, or the hide of a lion from his first stay in the tropics. Today, however, we have grown tired of such trophies, and even old hands and renowned big-game hunters have exchanged the telescopic sights and ammunition of their rifles for the bloodless weapon of the camera lens. One such hunter, who nevertheless shot a dozen leopards and a powerful bull elephant in his time, admitted to me: "I want to leave something for my children, something that is in danger of being lost: the living bush, inhabited by living animals...."

Chameleons. Drawing, 1869

JOURNEY
TO THE WATERFALLS

It was the young man's first journey to the interior of the land. Until now he had seen little more than a strip of coast and a handful of white men on the sisal plantation, and although he had learned how to ask for hot water or a lamp in the language of his native "boy," Nyuma, he still felt an outsider to the real life of the country.

They set out shortly after dawn. Herter, the gray-haired planter, had loaded up the high, metal-plated Ford with sacks and crates, and the boy and a black girl muffled up to her eyes in wraps were stowed away in the back. There the two shivered in the cool of the morning. The young man slipped a pistol hurriedly under the kapok cushion of the front seat. Herter probably saw him, but he said nothing.

The end of the brick-red soil marked the border of the plantation, and the banana trees and maize fields ceased with the last of the native huts. A few lean cattle stood in front of a mud wall, immobile as the two herders who tended them, leaning on long sticks as if they were spears. Constantly changing gear, Herter drove between bushes and termite hills out onto the steppe: a trackless plain covered with high yellow grass and broken by low hills and broad, flat-topped acacias beneath which the shadows cringed. The horizon, where a few mountains were still visible in the early morning, soon melted in the shimmering heat, and scorching columns of air danced over the battered hood of the Ford in the rocking rhythm of the drive.

And then the flies came. They stung the men and the girl in the face and nose, and there was no defense against them. To the young man's question, half curious and half anxious, as to whether it was true that the dreaded tsetse fly was to be found in the district, Herter replied: "Yes. But they are only dangerous to animals," and, after a sidelong glance, "There's no need to worry—anyway not about the flies." And again, after a pause: "You do take quinine?"

THE PICTURES:

Page 15	In the mountain regions of the Andes
Pages 16/17	Tropical rain forest near Machu Picchu, Peru
Pages 18/19	Leopard out for the kill
Pages 20/21	The Iguassu falls on the border of Argentina and Brazil
Page 22	Brood of small dragons: giant lizards

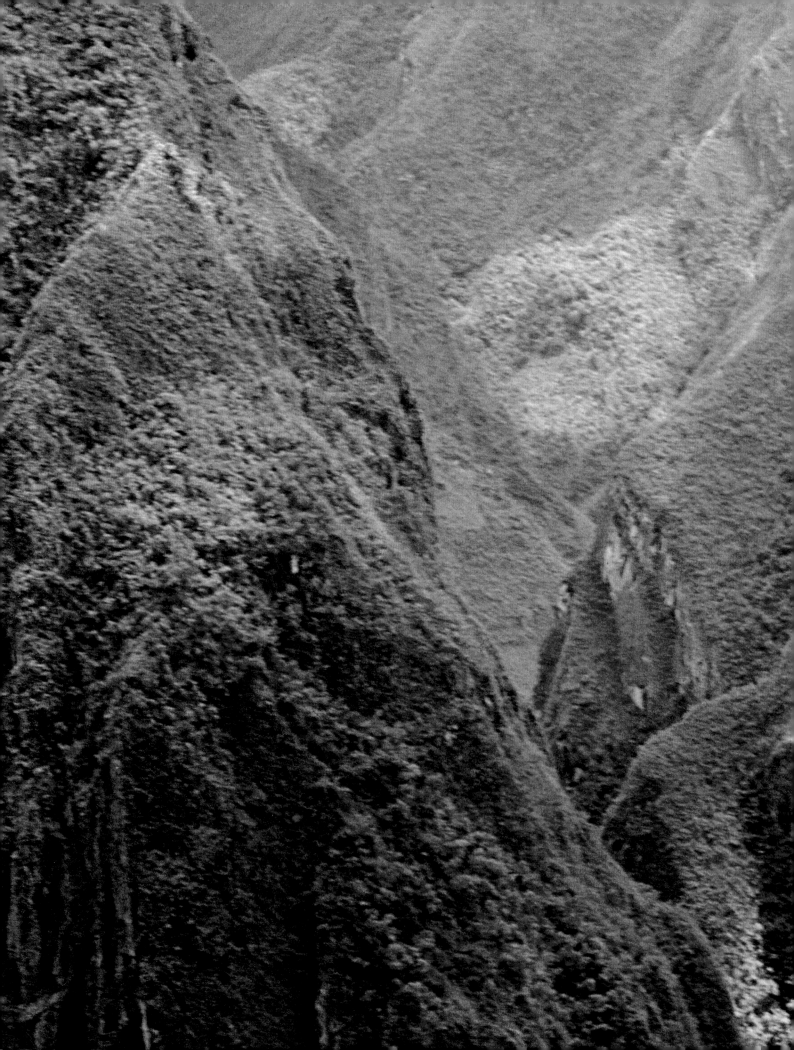

The young man nodded. Everyone on the plantation knew that Herter had caught malaria worse than anyone else and that he had an attack of fever almost every day. Once an attack had even knocked the tennis racket out of his hand in the middle of a game. Malaria had become part of his life, as weak lungs or whiskey or poker were for other men. He explained this to the young man, the newcomer, and a lot else besides. He talked of the importance of making the most of his time in the tropics and of getting away from the gossipy coastal community over weekends, of learning the language and of keeping a diary in order to be able to take something of value back to Europe when the time came, and to gain a criterion by which to judge his fellow men. Here in the wilderness the essence of a man was revealed, in his work and in his solitude, in the evening and at night. It was about all this, and more, that Herter spoke as they drove over the white-hot land, and about the black women, too.

At last they reached the gray-green tangle of a wood. It was nothing like the woods the young man was used to, for here was no pleasing, orderly array of tall, moss-covered trees bedecked with light whispering leaves. The light dropped like white wax onto the cracked earth from the gray web of the sparsely leaved branches overhead, and the Ford crawled wheezingly along, then came to a standstill. Unmoving, they listened to sounds that even Herter was unable to identify: was that the footfall of an animal, the scratching of a claw? A roving bird, or a lizard moving through the dead undergrowth?

The two men first noticed the troop of monkeys as their leader broke out of the bushes into the clearing. Upright and as tall as men, they stood grunting and baring their teeth and shaking their boar-like heads to and fro. Three or four of them took hold of branches and beat on the ground with them or held them like shields above their heads; others picked up stones and lumps of earth and flung them crookedly at the two men. As the young man reached for his gun, Herter laid his hand upon his arm and said simply: "No." He gripped the steering wheel with his right hand, and as the engine began to cough into life, the monkeys hurried over the clearing, leaping and jostling, screened by the still threatening older animals. Panting mothers carried their young on their backs, dozens and dozens of them, screaming hoarsely, their tails held aloft. Then they were lost

in the bushes, and their final barking was swallowed by a sudden silence as the car crawled on its way.

For hours the two men were lost in the confusion of impenetrable thornbushes, hard-baked lumps of earth, wide cracks in the ground, and sharp stones. Once Herter stopped to examine the droppings of a leopard. They were still quite fresh and lay in a half-dried-out creek in which, Nyuma maintained, there were fish. Would we let him set a few weir baskets in the hope of catching some? But his efforts met with no success, and the baskets brought no fish, no "delicious samaki," as Nyuma had prophesied.

After a final wheezing start the Ford reached the huts of a small village. The girl emerged suddenly from her wraps, leaped from the car, sped over the clearing, and disappeared into a hut. She had come on a visit, or maybe to bury her grandmother. Grandmothers always seemed to be dying in this country, and they were so alike that they might have been the same person, their names changing but never their honorable age and their habit of sudden death, a death which demanded a pious and respectful visit.

The sun was sinking, cutting ragged silhouettes out of the nearby mountains and the blue horizon across a narrow valley. With every foot that the car gained in height, something of the oppressiveness of the lowland fell away, and the leathery green vegetation along the road became a knotted, tangled forest that forced the track into a barely recognizable aisle and met over the heads of the intruders. The green-black dimness was filled with mist and drizzling rain.

They arrived at the lonely hotel, surrounded by ancient trees, shortly before the sudden fall of the African night. In the big, bleak, empty restaurant reddish lamps swam in the dimness of the chilly room. Silent waiters, barefoot and agile, appeared with food and softly clinking glasses, and the manager, a little old Goanese, stood silently in the background, giving wordless orders with his eyes.

The view from the wooden veranda, which leaned over the midnight-blue abyss of the mountain foothills, spread out over the soundless surf of the primeval forests into bottomless depths in which gleamed red eyes of distant fires. The trees that fingered the house with their branches exuded the scent of wild cinnamon. Gray baboons crouched motionless in the cool branches, clad in the shimmering white mantles of their hairy cowls, their forlorn eyes turned toward the house which was swallowed up in the night.

The young man, scared of the prospect of a hard, damp outdoor camp by the unexpected coolness of the night, went out on the deserted veranda and onto the brink of the night: the fires in the black abyss were extinguished, the whisper of the branches was silenced, and in its place arose a sound that he found it hard to place: soundlessly at first, the gray droplets of the night dew trickled from the green feathers of the trees, falling with a sigh from leaf to leaf into the abyss from which the nameless smell of night-green vegetation rose, stifling and almost unbearably oppressive. The stars were frozen in the cloudless night sky, and the ancient earth, divested of the cloak of time, held its breath in suspense.

On the following day the journey along the edge of the foothills led them past precipitous abysses in the steaming jungle, through dark, narrow tunnels of trees and the spray of cascading mountain streams, and out onto the road over the plain. They rolled and shook on under the glassy sky over steppes and sparse bush, crossed over dried-out river beds, climbed hills and slid down again toward the next deceptive creek. Hour after hour, stifled by the burden of the thrusting vertical light, they fought on like lost travelers. In the fifth hour of the afternoon the shade returned, growing out of the mango trees that reached up into the purple sky, creeping into the fields of manioc and maize where colorfully clad women toiled in the red glow of the setting sun, their forms melting into the veil of mist that hung over the silent steppe. Somewhat aloof, dominating the darkness so full of strange sounds, the mansion stood frozen in the cool blue of the twilight. The master of the house greeted the two travelers, invited them to sit down, filled their glasses. He listened smilingly to the young man's account of his experiences before nodding to the servant who was waiting with the news that the guests' baths were ready.

That night the young man wrote in his diary:

After dinner we sat on the veranda and discussed the events of the day. There was talk of clearance and new plantations, of machines and a projected field railway, of the natives in the camp and of a man who had disappeared with the gun of the monkey keeper and was now hiding in the bush. This had happened before, and the thief had always been found. But this time it was different, for

Baobabs, or monkey-bread trees, Africa

the man was mentally sick and roamed around at night imitating the roaring of a lion! The workers in the camp lived in constant fear of the madman, and our host had finally advised the government. The soldiers were expected to arrive that night.

Suddenly the yellow headlights of a car tore strips out of the darkness, there was a screech of brakes, and the brisk steps of an English officer rang out. Greetings were exchanged, glasses filled, and the officer enquired about the man

Tropical Scenery (Isle of Réunion)

THE PICTURES:

Page 27   Giraffe in Ngordoto, East Africa
Pages 28/29 Herd of elephants, Amboseli, East Africa
Pages 30/31 Well-protected curiosity: cheetah and her young
Pages 32/33 Excited bull elephant
Page 34   Jamaican forest
Page 35   The sloth
Pages 36/37 Lord of the jungle
Page 38   Hyena taken by surprise

they had come to arrest. The askaris were waiting in the second car, their eyes large and mute beneath their red fezzes. They were armed with rifles, and one of them was a sergeant.

We drove without lights and stopped at the edge of the camp to look for a path. A man crept out from the dark hollow of a hut and stood up; naturally he knew about the man who was possessed by a spirit and was out there in the bush. He refused to come with us, and disappeared into the night. Crouching shadows moved between the last huts, rising to their feet as we approached. Questions, whispering, questions. Then the truth emerged: the madman was the nephew of the man who had refused to come with us. A native pointed into the night and said: "He's out there! He can't be far. And he has a gun."

Suddenly the hungry cry of a lion out for the kill tore out of the gray confusion of the bush. We stood tense, silent and motionless, looking into the pale night, and again and again came the hoarse, hollow cry from the throat of a man who had become an animal. A young girl had followed us, and she stood among us

now, her eyes wide with fear, staring into the darkness and whispering a strangled, "No! No!" She was the young wife of the madman, who had beaten and tortured her before he had broken out into the night and become an animal. We left the askaris behind with the handcuffs and rifles. We all knew that he who roars like a lion has the strength of a lion. "We may have to kill him," said the sergeant. We could not get rid of the girl, who stood and stared into the night that hid her husband: a man lost forever, a man for whom rifles were waiting as for an animal. Rifles, handcuffs, and a cage.

The tiger's prey

They continued their journey the next day, Herter, the young man, and their host, setting out before dawn in their host's car in the cold, chalky light of the moon. After some trouble they found a track that wound between two mighty hills and lost itself in a treeless valley. A wall of reed-like grass, higher than a man, obstructed their view, and they left the car to search for a path in the thicket. The heat overtook them suddenly like a blow; foul odors rose from the decaying ground, and the sweat poured, smarting, over their backs and loins. Hornetlike insects stung their necks and hands, and blood ran over the young man's bare arms from the cuts that resulted from the merest touch of the knife-sharp elephant grass.

And then, in the distance, they heard a faint whisper that came and went in the banks of heat, returned, grew louder, increased to a murmur and finally to a softly rumbling thunder. And when, like exhausted swimmers, they reached the edge of the foul-smelling hollow, stumbling and panting, they encountered cold banks of mist to which they thankfully offered their arms and chests, staggering on toward the clearing and the awe-inspiring abyss that forced them to a standstill. From the green matted walls of a huge hollow, white waters broke from a hundred sources, tumbled in cascades from depth to depth, and became one with the rumbling thunder of the abyss from which the waters, scattered into spray, foamed up and sank like a veil onto the green floor of the jungle. Over the craggy circle of the boiling cauldron hung a rainbow—a colored arc of light, gleaming, soft, and weightless. And the gentle flying spray moistened the ground like a dew, making a pure, cool carpet of green scattered with delicate pink flowers. To the three silent men, it was as if no human foot had ever before ventured into this seclusion, and their hearts were filled with a nameless awe.

THE BLACK BUTTERFLY

My friends on the plantation in Pangani had talked so much about old Krugher and his stories during our evening conversations that I decided to visit him. If what they said was true, it seemed that he must have either an exceptional talent for telling tales or an impressive collection of African stories which, as he said himself, had somehow gathered together inside him. I was also told, however, that it was not easy either to find him on his coffee plantation or, once found, to get him to talk. He was a strange man, and hard of hearing as well. I had some trouble finding a guide willing to come with me, for the plantation was situated far from the coast in the midst of wild bush-land, and the natives told terrible tales of leopards which roamed the district in broad daylight and which had stolen all the cattle and goats of the natives who once lived there. It seemed that Krugher lived alone with an old, one-eyed attendant who slept under his employer's bed—that is, if he slept at all, for it was said that Krugher's hut had no door, no bars on the windows, and no fence.

When I reached the plantation after an eight-hour journey through the bush and steppe and a forest of wild rubber trees as still as the grave, there was no one to be seen and no sound anywhere. The skins of two giant crocodiles and the toothless skull of an elephant lay on the stone veranda, and a carved stick of the kind carried in their right hands by native chiefs at tribal meetings leaned against a forsaken rocking chair. All my shouts and calls were in vain. No one came and nothing happened. Strangely enough, the small coffee plantation was well kept and seemed quite prosperous.

On my third visit to the plantation it was quite a shock to find Krugher sitting in his rocking chair, obviously waiting for me, and I had the feeling that I had seen him somewhere before. It did not occur to me that he simply fitted to perfection the picture I had made of him. He was tall, lean, and white-haired, and he had a long mustache like

THE PICTURES:

Page 41	Trees covered with Spanish moss in the Florida Everglades
Pages 42/43	Lynx on a high plateau bordering the Grand Canyon
Pages 44/45	Baby lion in a bad mood
Page 46	Coral snake
Page 47	Green tree snake, Malaya
Page 48	Young zebra in flight
Page 49	Pair of rhinoceroses
Pages 50/51	Baboon with impalas in the background
Page 52	Tender and concerned mother baboon

a Chinese mandarin or a nineteenth-century general, and the dim eyes of a man who is used to staring into the fire or the setting sun.

He seemed to know why I had come and that I had brought a new roller for his oil press. Friends had asked me to bring it with me. He took it with a nod and conveyed his thanks and best wishes to my friends, whom he believed he had not seen for more than four years. In the course of conversation I learned that he had not been to the harbor town of Tanga for a long time, that he possessed no car, read no newspapers, and received no visitors. He was too old for almost everything, he said; besides, he was content with what he had, and he waved vaguely in the direction of the trees and bushes and the clearing in which his plantation lay.

"Since I lost my wife..."

"Since you...?"

But he offered no further explanation, and after a long pause he wiped his thoughts from his wrinkled brow with the back of his hand and said: "Come on a Saturday. Do come on a Saturday. Then we shall have more time and I shall be able to tell you something about this country, since it seems to interest you."

Lion monkeys, drawing, 1872

I saw him many times after this, and we talked about all sorts of things: about wild animals, about the crocodiles he had shot. Yes, and the elephants too. But that was a long time ago, and it had cost him a lot of money and a lot of patience—patience in dealing with the district game warden, because he had no license. "But what else could I do when the elephants trampled all over the plantation at night and ate the maize—what would *you* have done?"

The stories came much later. He had been speaking about World War I and about how the Germans had held the English in check for four years, including the fleet which continually bombarded the coast. "We used to sit under dug-out termite hills and listen to the scream of the bullets. They lost about ten thousand horses which they had brought up from the Nile—they died by the thousands like the wajaggas which came down from Kilimanjaro and died of a wrong diet. It was hardly surprising, for they were banana eaters and were hardly likely to thrive on tinned meat."

After a pause: "Africa is a hard country. For white men, too, planters and hunters. I have known many who could not survive in the bush. Most of them drank themselves to death, sitting alone with the bottle on their plantations for months on end. Some of them started beating their servants or their workers or their native women—whom they couldn't talk to—and this was often the first step toward the grave. One man was killed by a rhinoceros, even though he managed to get into his car. It simply crushed him between the seat and the radiator, like a locomotive.... Then there was the Swede who always wore high boots—a good drinker. He often used to come here and sit where you are sitting now. I told him many times not to rest his arms on the railings, but he didn't listen, and one day a black mamba bit him in the hand. We hadn't any serum at the time, and although the boy sucked the wound, it didn't do any good.

"Once the locusts came. Suddenly they were here, the whole sky full of them, so thick you couldn't see the sun. It was like a sandstorm. They settled on everything in sight, ate the plantation bare, and moved on like a steamroller. There was nothing left when they had finished, no leaves, no growth of any kind. At first the natives tried to frighten them off by shouting and beating on metal cans with sticks, but they gave up after a while and caught and roasted the fattest ones instead; we were soon sick of the smell and taste of them. Three days later it was all over. They had eaten the land bare. It was a huge swarm, eighty miles wide, maybe ten miles long, and three to four yards deep. Three whole days. Then there were the ants, the siafu. They came at night. I had a few ducks at the time, and some tame antelopes enclosed by a high wire fence; and a young leopard, too, in a cage with bars. Here on the veranda. It must have been the whining and squealing that woke me—the ants were everywhere. The ducks were running about like mad things—the ants were already in their eyes. The little bush bucks, too, and the leopard. The cage was black with ants, and the leopard raved and roared and screamed like a thing possessed. We couldn't open the cage—we couldn't find the key. And then they came onto us. At first we only felt a crawling sensation, until they reached our hips. Then they started using their pincers, hundreds of them, all at once, and it was no use brushing them off because the pincers remained in the flesh like clamps. It was enough to drive you crazy. We ran and hopped and jumped like dancing dervishes. We threw the antelopes into the big water tank, but it was too late—they were already blind. I shot the leopard in the end, in his cage. And then we left for the next plantation, the men and the

women and the children and me, in pairs and threesomes, on bicycles. "The first thing we did was to have a drink and change our clothes. The next day the ants had gone. Only the bones and the horns of the antelopes were left on the plantation, and most of the cans in the kitchen were empty—they had bored holes and eaten the contents. The whole house was bare, stripped clean: no spiders, no beetles, no snakes, no geckos. Bado Kufa was still alive then. He was my best boy; he never told lies, and I didn't grudge him the few cigarettes he pinched from my supplies. One day he went down to the river to wash some clothes. You know how they do it, crouching by the water and beating and kneading the soapy clothing on a stone. His screams could be heard as far away as the farthest huts. His whole lower jaw had gone, torn away by a crocodile which had taken him by surprise. And all the time he screamed, "Bado Kufa! Bado Kufa!" which, roughly translated, means "Not dead yet!" He had saved his life by pressing his thumbs into the crocodile's eyes and hanging on until the beast tore itself away and swam off—with Bado Kufa's jaw. Our cook, Mali ya mbibi, patched him up. He knew something about everything—he was a real miracle doctor. Four days later Bado Kufa turned up to work as if nothing had happened. Bado Kufa..."

Reptiles fighting

Krugher let the name ring on in the silence and searched his memory for something lost, forgotten. When he began to talk again, his manner seemed somehow more cautious. "I don't think they exist any longer, boys like Bado Kufa, Mali ya mbibi, or Saidi. Of course, they were paid for their pains, twenty rupees a year maybe, and food and a piece of the plantation and a few yards of material for their wives. But I paid them according to their faithfulness, not their work. Saidi was different: mentally, he was a child, but he was a giant of strength, and completely fearless. Once he appeared with a dead leopard slung around his shoulders like a sack. The animal had made the mistake of thinking that it could steal Saidi's goats and go unpunished! Saidi waited for it at the spot where it came up from the river in the evening and killed it with his bare hands, breaking its skull with his blows. Mali ya mbibi said that Saidi had been helped by spirits, but Saidi told him he would do better to look for ghosts in his own cooking pots, or elsewhere. The 'elsewhere' probably referred to the cook's hut around which two-legged ghosts often used to creep, for Mali ya mbibi was old, fat, and childless. But Saidi was secretly afraid of Mali ya mbibi's culinary skill, for it was said that his cooking had mysteriously disagreed with his rich uncle.... Once, as I was waiting for friends who were coming to dinner, I sent Saidi down to the pump by the river, which drove our small dynamo. It was a lousy pump and was always going on strike. That night, however, the lights shone with uninterrupted brilliance, for when the pump stopped, Saidi drove the dynamo with his own hands. Saidi..."

Krugher's one-eyed attendant approached us silently and waited for Krugher to look up. "The *mshenzi* is here again," he said.

And it was a wretched being which now came forward into the light, a black heap of misery, trembling all over, although it was not cold. "Fever," said Krugher, and told the old man to give him the small brown bottle of white pills. He counted out three of them into the twitching hand of the terrified native who tossed them into his toothless mouth, swallowed them, threw up his hands, stared at Krugher with his yellow eyes—and was gone.

"Daniel was not always a *mshenzi*," said Krugher. "The natives from the *mporini*, the bush, are known as washenzis, and they are completely ignorant, unable to read or count up to ten. Most of them have neither wives nor land, and they live from hand to mouth. You might say that they are primitive, but in all the fifty years that I've been living here I've never known anyone who was really primitive....

"Daniel used to be one of the best trackers, and he often used to accompany me. He could never get used to a gun and relied on his bow and arrow to shoot monkeys, bush bucks, and guinea fowl. Apparently he once even killed a lion. It was Daniel who went out with young Bruce. Bruce was the craziest character I ever met. He came out here to sell petrol, lubricating oil, tools, and pumps. He soon got acclimatized, and he slept in the native camps or the car or his sleeping bag or on the grass. And he chased butterflies. In the English club in Mombasa bets were made of five, ten, and a hundred pounds as to whether he would catch it—the black butterfly with the two mother-of-pearl spots on its wings. There was a woman in the story—one of those young, spoiled, coveted, and heartless women who do not bother to think what they are doing when they whisper to a man: 'I want a diamond! Or a dozen leopard skins! Or—a black butterfly! Black as black velvet. Get it for me, honey....' And so Bruce set out to hunt the black butterfly. For two long years." Krugher

THE PICTURES:

Pages 57, 58/59, 60
The Erigpagtsá Indians
of Brazil

56

was silent. The night wind sighed through the bougainvillea bushes, dropped, and fell asleep. The mad laughter of a hyena came out of the black of the night and died away again. Time trickled away like sand in an hourglass.

"Bruce came here often, and I was always glad to see him. We were living lonely lives then, and I was glad to have him in the house when I went into town or up into the mountains. At that time I was trying to cultivate a plantation of oil-palms—with a singular lack of success, by the way. Then the war came. My wife, who died of malaria the same year, saw Bruce last. He acted very strange, she said, and he seemed confused and very tired. He left once more for the great swamp, taking Daniel with him. Daniel watched Bruce sink in the swamp, slowly and silently, the green butterfly net held aloft above his head."

On my last visit to Krugher he pressed a cigarette box into my hand without a word. On the yellowed cotton wool from a medicine bottle, disintegrating, gray, and lifeless lay the torn wings of a butterfly which must have once been black.

JUNGLE FEVER

The men of the past whose life work and aim were the discovery and exploration of unknown lands and their peoples, environments, and cultures were always to a certain extent outsiders. In order to liberate themselves from a constraint which arrested the development of their unusual personalities, they were forced to seek new and wider horizons. This urge to break away from their mental, moral, or political bondage had various causes, among them background, education, and character, but in most cases, although the results of their endeavors are revealed in the testimony of factual reports, the motivating urge remains a mystery.

Of course, I am not talking of the adventurers, profiteers, and villains who terrorized whole continents in the role of unscrupulous successors to the sixteenth-century conquistadors. No, I mean the men who set out much later with the aim of giving spiritual aid to the descendants of the "savages" who had survived the first Christian invasion. And I also mean the men who set out to seek lost civilizations, some of them missionaries—if by missionaries we mean men of faith and renunciation; and others fanatics—if we ascribe a certain spiritual and moral merit to fanatiscism.

David Livingstone, who was born in Blantyre Works in Scotland in 1813, is generally regarded as the prototype of the missionary in the nineteenth-century sense of the word, not merely because of the fact that the London Missionary Society sent the twenty-eight-year-old theologian and doctor out to the Kuruman Mission Station on the edge of the Kalahari Desert in 1840, but because he was a deeply devout, deeply charitable, yet thoroughly modern man who perceived and responded to the call of the Dark Continent and the physical wretchedness of its people. His abortive journey, perilous yet rich in geographical discoveries, lasted for eleven years and led him to Luanda in the west and Quelimane in the east, made him the first

The caravan approaches

European to visit the Victoria Falls in 1855, and finally came to an end in Tanganyika. To the natives on his missionary station he was minister, teacher, doctor, and adviser. His readiness to help, his unshakable faith in a better future, and the kindness in his eyes won him the respect and trust of even the tribal chiefs; in addition, he was a secret conspirator against one of the greatest evils in the land—slave trading.

After thirty years of searching and fighting, however, he was, in his own words, sick, desperately tired, and sad. This lone wolf who was not spared even the Biblical fate of falling among thieves (his entire property and possessions were stolen from him in 1866 when he was erroneously reported dead) had yet another experience in store: his meeting with Henry Morton Stanley who had been sent out by the *New York Herald* to find the missing missionary, and who, on finding the legendary figure, stammered: "I thank God, Doctor, I have been permitted to see you." This was on November 10, 1871, in a native village called Udjidji northwest of Lake Tanganyika. Two years later the pilgrimage of this true disciple of Christ ended in Chitambo, some distance farther on. In the dawn of May 1, 1873, his servants found their master kneeling before his camp bed, his head held in his hands, fallen asleep for the last time in prayer.

The following account may perhaps seem too fantastic to be true, but it nevertheless contributes to an understanding of the personality and fate of a most unusual man, the English colonel P. H. Fawcett, who disappeared on a search for a forgotten civilization in the Brazilian jungle in the 1920s.

Only twenty-four years after Columbus had discovered the New World, the sixteenth-century Portuguese adventurer Diego Alvarez was stranded on the coast of Brazil at the point where Bahia now stands, in the territory of the cannibalistic Tupinamba Indians. The fact that he was not eaten was probably due less to the strangeness of his appearance than to the fact that an Indian girl named Paraguassa took a fancy to him and became his wife. The Portuguese mariner lived with the Indians for many years, established friendly relations with them, and even succeeded in converting Paraguassa to Christianity. One of her sisters then married another Portuguese adventurer whose son, Melchior·Dias Moreya, spent most of his life with the Indians and was known to them as Muribeca. He discovered many mines and accumulated vast quantities of silver, gold, and precious stones. His son, Roberio Dias, approached the Portuguese king, Dom Pedro II, with an offer to hand over the mines in exchange for the title of Marquis das Minas, but the king was too cunning for him and he paid for his mistake by two years in prison. Having bought his freedom for 9000 crowns, he died in 1622, and the secret of the mines was never disclosed.

In the following three decades the search for the lost mines cost many lives, the adventurers falling prey to fever, snakes, wild animals, poisonous spiders, alligators, hunger, thirst and madness. Solitary adventurers, groups of explorers, and "Bandeiras," or Flags, as the officially sponsored expeditions accompanied by government troops and a contingent of missionaries were called, tried their luck to no avail.

Colonel Fawcett, D.S.O., English officer, explorer, ethnographer, surveyor, and gentleman, was not only familiar with the stories and speculations about the mines of Muribeca; he had also come across an old document from 1743 in which a native of Minas Gerais, whom Fawcett calls Francisco Raposo, reports on an ancient, deserted, and mysterious city, half strangled by the jungle, which he and his Bandeiras had discovered. Colonel Fawcett, to whom reports of forgotten civilizations in the jungles of the Amazon were nothing new, was particularly intrigued by a passage in Raposo's account in which he mentioned "white people" with long black hair whom his scouting party had caught sight of in a canoe. Fawcett described the route which he took on his search for this lost civilization in letters and diaries written in the language common to great explorers which often reads more like a prophecy than a factual report. In his book entitled *Exploration Fawcett,* the explorer's son Brian gives an account of his father's well-nigh inexplicable odyssey, but basically the book is an

THE PICTURES:

Page 65   Yaguas Indian on a branch
            of the Amazon in Peru
Page 66   Nile crocodile
Page 67   Watchful hippopotamuses
Page 68   *Above:* Colorful tropical
            starling
            Left: Pink flamingo
            Right: Herons
Page 69   Secretary birds cleaning
            their feathers
Pages 70/71 Flamingos in flight
Page 72   *Above, left, and below:*
            Tropical flowers
            Right: Flower and fruit
            of the mango
Page 73   Bird of paradise plant
            in the Brazilian jungle
Page 74   Above the timberline
            of Mount Kenya,
            East Africa

almost tragic monologue by a man who sacrificed nineteen years of his life to an idea. Fawcett really believed in the existence of this highly civilized city somewhere in the heart of the Brazilian jungle— for nineteen long years!

On May 29, 1925, he wrote his last words to his wife: "You need have no fear of any failure," and the monologue comes to an abrupt end. Whether Fawcett and his eldest son were shot or attacked by hostile Indians, as was rumored, or whether they in fact arrived at their goal and became one with the great silence is not known. Maybe one of the Kalapalo Indians in the Xingu region of the Brazilian jungle preserves the secret?

Sometimes those obsessed by the urge to discover, to whom we give the somewhat naïve name of explorers, have luck on their side. On the last day of an almost despairing search for traces of old civilizations in Petén, Guatemala, among the poisonous vermin of tropical creeping plants, an explorer called Pierre Ivanoff came across a carved stone which led to the discovery of a burial ground and the walls and portals of sacred buildings, witnesses of a lost city unknown even to the heathen Chiapos, descendants of the Mayas, who lived so close to the temples of their ancestors and their gods. An archaeologist estimated these findings to have dated from the eighth century A.D., from a time when Europe was barely civilized and liberated from heathen practices. Was it sickness or earthquakes that extinguished the life of the city? Or was it condemned to die by the avenging wilderness?

Time is not important in the jungle and the bush, a fact illustrated by this extract from a letter from a planter in the Congo:

Since I last wrote, I have lost my calendar or given it to the mission, and I am far from sure about the passing of time. But it doesn't matter in the least. Thank you for your concern, but my attack of malaria was not too bad. Nevertheless, I am going to Ndele tomorrow, for it seems that there are ancient dancing masks there and a native who knows how to banish fever....

THE SAVAGES

It is idle to ask when Europeans first gave the name of savages to the human beings whom they met on their voyages of discovery to the Dark Continent and the coasts of the newly discovered continents in the west. The Indians who were amenable to their Christian conquerors in recognition of the religious character of their mission were not savages but were regarded as such because they were "heathens" and unbaptized and were therefore treated as inferior beings who had no right to understanding or consideration. It is questionable whether any real racial problems existed at the time; certainly a distinction was made between brown, black, and yellow, but it was probably only those who by virtue of their unfamiliar way of living, thinking, and feeling were deemed primitive who were looked upon as savages, and centuries had to pass before Europeans made any attempt to understand their way of life. These peoples were not regarded as fellow human beings but as strange, unintelligible, and sometimes hostile creatures and were treated as chattels, like ivory, spices, rubber, tobacco, and the skins of animals. As late as the nineteenth century the slave trade with black Africa was still a reputable, if inhuman, business.

But the natives of the African jungle, the tropical jungles of South America, the undiscovered wilderness of Borneo and of central Australia were never really primitive at all. They were, and are, simply different and remain misunderstood to this day. It was only when the white man became aware of his own hidden and suppressed instincts—wars, sickness, and inexplicable cultural crises may have contributed to this self-knowledge—that he began to investigate the lives and minds of those peoples who, almost like relics of bygone eras, led enigmatic lives on the borders of his civilization. As late as 1646 a man employed by a Netherlands East India company reported after a three-day stay in Cape Province in Africa that the natives,

Rope bridge of the Brazilian Indians

although they resembled human beings in appearance, were more similar to animals in their morals and way of life, and one of his contemporaries considered that they bore more resemblance to monstrous apes than to human beings.

When the "savages," who for a long time appeared in literature as a kind of wild animal, finally lost something of the inhumanity ascribed to them, they still continued to be labeled "devilish," "rascally," and "heathen" by many missionaries and literary world travelers who, armed to the teeth with weapons and prejudice, dared to penetrate to the edge of the wilderness. After all, most of them were believed to be cannibals, head hunters, drug-addicted magicians, or leopard-men who mutilated their fellow tribesmen! Even Robinson Crusoe's companion, his "Man Friday," had cannibals as his ancestors, and it seemed only right and proper to the readers of this fascinating book about the wilderness that Robinson Crusoe should have used his gun. It was not until the age of romanticism that the "noble" savage was discovered, the brave, fearless, and trustworthy redskin who—and this was Rousseau's idea—fought the paleface only to preserve his freedom and his ancestral hunting grounds. But the situation regarding the cannibals and the Australian natives was still not clear, and cannibalism was not regarded as extinct even in our century. I remember a memorandum which appeared in a West African newspaper about 1930 which reported that unknown members of a "savage tribe" had "killed, cooked, and eaten" a white man, whereupon an English colonial official and cynic expressed the opinion that it was a comfort to know that the man had been killed first and cooked and eaten afterward. Incidentally, serious research has shown that cannibalism has its roots in magic, for enemies killed in battle as well as certain fellow tribesmen were eaten only in order that their strength and abilities might be passed on to the living. And that which we regard as superstition is basically a belief in the elemental power of the soul, and thus in eternal life.

It will probably be some time yet before it is generally realized that historical and ethnographical knowledge is not sufficient for an understanding of the turning points and crises in the spiritual development of the young African countries; it is also necessary to make a study of the mental make-up of the peoples, formed as they are by their elemental religions, in order to comprehend their essential beings. Misunderstood peoples are always a political and an ideological danger—even for old Europe!

I remember the words of a very unusual man who lived for many years among the Australian aborigines:

I do not consider these people, who are used to being classified through arrogance and ignorance as relics of the Stone Age, to be at all primitive in the sense of being simple-minded. When I succeeded in overcoming their shyness and reluctance to talk—which they consider to be a virtually punishable surrender of their knowledge—I realized how deep and many-sided they really are. The knowledge they gain through experience, for example about the weather and hunting, is backed up by instincts and presentiments and the magical powers which they regard as an inseparable part of nature, and all-embracing. But it was their art, and above all their portrayals of animals and the spirits of the dead, which really made me aware that they live in constant communication with the Universal Spirit which permeates all things and beings. It was only later that I realized that the European Ice-Age man, whom no one has described as primitive, produced similar images of magical practices and spirits and of hunting scenes ten, twenty, or fifty thousand years previously.

It may be this parallel which makes us speak of the aborigines as a race which has remained at the same stage of development as Stone Age man. But we have not the right to maintain that these people are devoid of any culture, even if it does appear to be on a lesser scale than that of other, more developed primitives races among whom, incidentally, there still exist tribes which light their daily fires by rubbing two sticks together. It is the huge isolation in which the native inhabitants of Australia still live that has hindered their development, a development which, after all, is made possible only through contact with other tribes and peoples. For many primitive races, however, a certain

THE PICTURES:

Page 79   In the West Nigerian rain forests
Pages 80/81   In the swamps of the Everglades
Page 82   Moonrise in the tropical bush

78

isolation in space and time may be considered a stroke of fortune, for otherwise they would have come into unavoidable contact with a thoughtless and materialistic civilization and long since have become extinct. The case of the North American Indians, robbed of their rightful environment, reduced, and finally enclosed in reservations, is a sad enough example. Civilizations do not perish through wars, hostile attacks, epidemics, and natural catastrophes alone, even though they may be the instrument of the disappearance of tribes, clans, and races; the destruction of the spiritual and moral law and order that holds a society together and gives it stability and strength is the final criterion. But does not such law and order exist among the so-called primitive peoples? Do the Bambute pygmies in the Congolese jungle, the Waura Indians of Brazil, the Kenyah in Borneo, and the Haida in British Columbia—to mention only a few of the last surviving peoples of antiquity—really live their lives free from compulsion and constraint, lives in which the semblance of law and order is based only on the battle for naked existence, as is sometimes still believed today?

Thorough, unprejudiced modern investigation teaches us differently, for it not only dispenses with the false image of insensible, indifferent savages living in a net of incomprehensible taboos and arbitrary actions of despotic chiefs, it also shows us that their lives are in fact conducted within systems of law and order and flexible and considered conventions—systems which, although they are strictly hierarchical, nevertheless ensure each member the right to his individuality, a right which may be publicly defended if necessary. Since their laws, like the economically necessary obligations of the tribe and clan, are barely or not at all set down in writing, the necessity of a revision of binding norms constantly arises. These people, too, know crime, punishment, and atonement—and this may even take the form of suicide in cases of adultery. So it is hardly surprising that the post-mortem examination is an accepted means of jurisdiction when a magician oversteps the mark....

These, then, are the "savages."

Campfires

THE WILDERNESS AS REFUGE

The probability of encountering a family of gorillas in the heart of the tropical jungle is, even today, not very big, despite local guidance by safari guides and practiced hunters. At least these most nearly human of all primates have been provided by nature with a relatively inaccessible environment which is essential for the preservation of the species. The wilderness which has not yet been destroyed by man is a natural reservation in which the old animal world has found a refuge and where vegetation in which this fauna can live and reproduce is plentiful. The extinction of this flora and fauna would result in an impoverishment and finally in the complete loss of the natural order of things and would dangerously alter the image of our earth in an ecological sense. The danger that threatens this natural order is greater than can be conceived of by a largely urban society, but it is the human being imprisoned in his industrialized and technological environment who should take an interest in the preservation of this last paradise, for it could become a refuge when the urge comes over him to flee from the oppressive narrowness and lack of freedom of his everyday life. The realization that a return to nature is beneficial to our psychological well-being and a breath of life to our stunted spirits has led to an attempt to safeguard these oases of natural recovery. The number of wild reserves, of natural parks and animal reservations which have come into being in the twentieth century alone is satisfyingly large; even more gratifying is the generosity with which, in the United States, for example, the government, often faced with the opposition of materialistic circles, has created huge natural reservations in which man may be a guest but may on no account try his hand at trapping or shooting the wild animals. Canada is another example of generous natural preservation, and the reservations in the Congo and South Africa have for decades been some of the greatest attractions for animal lovers. Recently the governments of the newer

Under the giant redwoods of the
Sierra Nevada, California, 1885

African states have realized that good business can be done with the wilderness: roaring lions, trumpeting elephants, snorting hippopotamuses, photogenic giraffes, and elegant leopards—not to mention campfires, glowing sunsets, and ice-cold whisky!

Disfiguration of the wilderness? An insult to nature? Anyone whose eyes and heart have been opened to a new and hitherto unknown world by his first fleeting contact with the tropics and who has felt the feverish compulsion to penetrate deeper into the interior of a land that has miraculously remained mysterious will always find taciturn and tenacious companions to show him the way into the great adventure of the wilderness. It is an adventure that can easily take an unexpected turn and lead the discovery-happy visitor onto a track that may take him not to big game, lions, and campfires in the jungle but deeper and deeper into the wilderness: namely to man, to real contact with the natives. Sometimes even their language may become accessible, and the benefit gained from knowledge of a local language is inestimably greater than any hunting trophies. More than one traveler in Africa has discovered the fascination of, for example, Kiswaheli, the language of the Waswahili and other East African tribes, which is full of nuances and images. It not only has more grammatical cases than most European languages (locative and vocative); it is also exceedingly vivid in its symbolism—thus for example "mtoto" (the child), and "meza" (the table) combine to make "mtoto ya meza" (the drawer). But the wilderness is also the last refuge of the peoples we have driven from their hunting grounds, from their ancient hiding places, to the edge of civilization. Men from the bush, from the night-dark forests, from the security of forgottenness. And perhaps some still remain to this day, living undisturbed on islands marked on no map, in caves on the slopes of rugged mountains, or in clearings by rivers that have no beginning and no name.

PHOTOGRAPHERS   Toni Angermayer 69

Ulfert Beckert 16/17

Brian Brake 10

BUNTE/Mörk 34

Hans Dossenbach 12, 15, 18/19,
  22, 32/33, 41, 44/45, 46, 47, 48,
  50/51, 66, 67, 68, 70/71,
  72 *above, middle left, below,* 74,
  80/81, 82

Peter A. Feer 28/29

foto-present 20/21

E. A. Heiniger 42/43

Harald Mante 27

Lott Meyerlist 49

Oestman/J. R. Simon 35

Gordon Parks 36/37

PHOTO RESEARCHERS/
  Trevor 30/31, Peterson 38

SATOUR 52

Emil Schulthess 65, 73

Harald Schultz 11, 57, 58/59, 60

Picture archives Kh. Schuster/
Hoffmann-Burchardi 79

Walter Wissenbach 9

Central Color Picture Archives 72
  middle right

Cover picture:
  PHOTO RESEARCHERS/
  Simon Trevor: Cheetah and
  her young

Vignettes on pages:
  6/7, 13, 24/25, 39, 53, 54/55,
  76/77, and 85 from originals
  from the PTT Museum, Berne,
  Switzerland

References to passages
in Lieutenant Colonel
P. H. Fawcett's Exploration
Fawcett in the chapter
"Jungle Fever" by kind
permission of the Hutchinson
Publishing Group Ltd., London